Pebble®

Out in Space

The Sun

by Martha E. H. Rustad

Consulting Editor: Gail Saunders-Smith, PhD

Consultant: Roger D. Launius, PhD
Senior Curator, Division of Space History
National Air and Space Museum
Smithsonian Institution, Washington, D.C.

Capstone
press®

Mankato, Minnesota

Pebble Books are published by Capstone Press,
151 Good Counsel Drive, P.O. Box 669, Mankato, Minnesota 56002.
www.capstonepress.com

1 2 3 4 5 6 13 12 11 10 09 08

Library of Congress Cataloging-in-Publication Data
Rustad, Martha E. H. (Martha Elizabeth Hillman), 1975–
    The sun / by Martha E.H. Rustad. — Pebble rev. and updated [ed.]
    p. cm. — (Pebble Books. Out in space)
    Summary: "Simple text and photographs introduce the Sun and its
features" — Provided by publisher.
    Includes bibliographical references and index.
    ISBN-13: 978-1-4296-1721-5 (hardcover)
    ISBN-10: 1-4296-1721-7 (hardcover)
    ISBN-13: 978-1-4296-2837-2 (softcover)
    ISBN-10: 1-4296-2837-5 (softcover)
    1. Sun — Juvenile literature. I. Title.
QB521.5.R87 2009
523.7 — dc22   2007051432

Note to Parents and Teachers

The Out in Space set provides the most up-to-date solar system
information to support national science standards. This book
describes and illustrates the Sun. The photographs support early
readers in understanding the text. This book also introduces early
readers to subject-specific vocabulary words, which are defined
in the Glossary section. Early readers may need assistance to read
some words and to use the Table of Contents, Glossary, Read More,
Internet Sites, and Index sections of the book.

Table of Contents

A Yellow Star

The Sun shines
brightly in the sky.
It is a yellow star.

The Sun is the
closest star to Earth.
It is 93 million miles
(150 million kilometers)
away from Earth.

The Sun is like
other stars in space.
It is a burning ball
of gases.

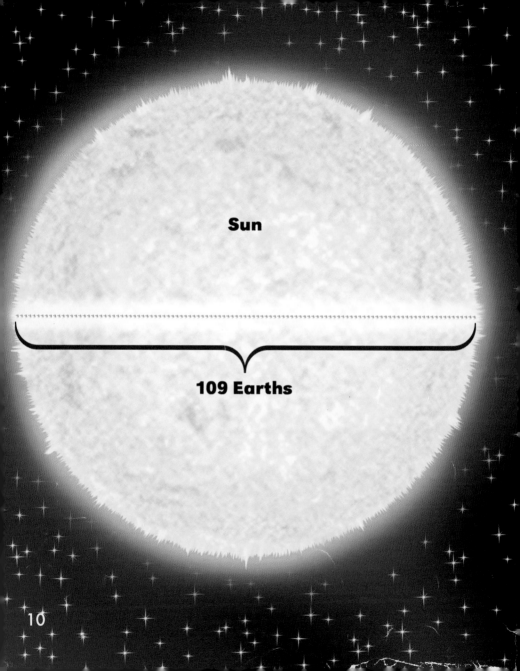

Sun

109 Earths

The Sun is much
larger than Earth.
About 109 Earths
could fit across
the Sun.

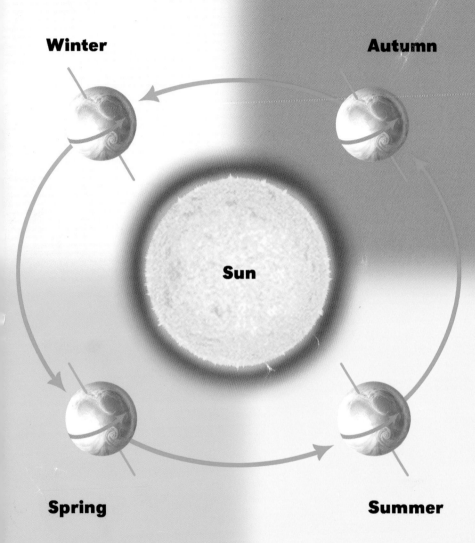

Winter

Autumn

Sun

Spring

Summer

14

Earth moves around
the Sun once each year.
The seasons change
as Earth moves
around the Sun.

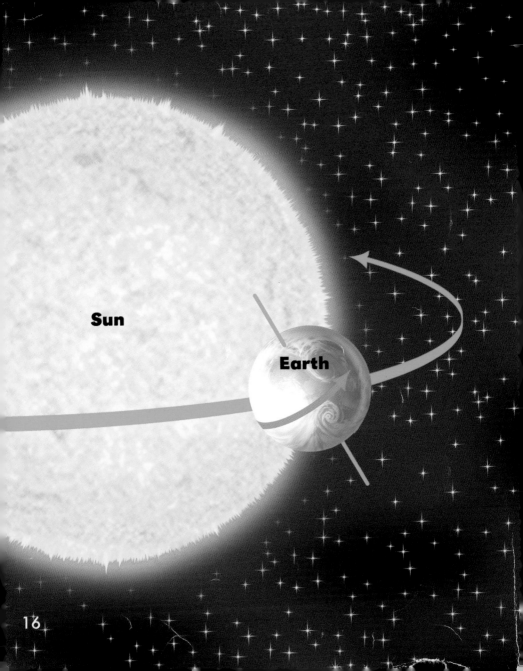

Sun

Earth

The Sun in Earth's Sky

Earth spins
once each day.
As Earth spins,
the Sun seems to
move across the sky.

The Sun rises in the east every morning. The Sun sets in the west every night.

The Sun gives Earth
light and heat.
The Sun makes
life on Earth possible.

Glossary

asteroid — a large rocky body that moves around the Sun; asteroids are too small to be called planets.

comet — a ball of rock and ice that moves around the Sun

dwarf planet — a round object that moves around the Sun but is too small to be a planet; Pluto is a dwarf planet.

gas — a substance that spreads to fill any space that holds it; the Sun is made of hydrogen and helium gases.

planet — a large object that moves around the Sun

solar system — the Sun and the objects that move around it; our solar system has eight planets, dwarf planets including Pluto, and many moons, asteroids, and comets.

yellow star — a medium-sized star; the Sun is a yellow star.

Read More

Adamson, Thomas K. *The Sun.* Exploring the Galaxy. Mankato, Minn.: Capstone Press, 2007.

Bailey, Jacqui. *Sun Up, Sun Down: The Story of Day and Night.* Science Works. Minneapolis: Picture Window Books, 2004.

Bredeson, Carmen. *What Do You Know about the Sun?* I Like Space! Berkeley Heights, N.J.: Enslow, 2008.

Internet Sites

FactHound offers a safe, fun way to find Internet sites related to this book. All of the sites on FactHound have been researched by our staff.

Here's how:

1. Visit *www.facthound.com*

2. Choose your grade level.

3. Type in this book ID **1429617217** for age-appropriate sites. You may also browse subjects by clicking on letters, or by clicking on pictures and words.

4. Click on the **Fetch It** button.

FactHound will fetch the best sites for you!

Index

Word Count: 143
Grade: 1
Early-Intervention Level: 14

Editorial Credits
Katy Kudela, revised edition editor; Kim Brown, designer and illustrator;
    Jo Miller, photo researcher

Photo Credits
Getty Images Inc./All Canada Photos/John E. Marriott, 4; NASA/JPL, 12
(Neptune and Venus); NASA/STScI, 12 (Jupiter and Saturn); NASA/USGS, 12
(Mars and Uranus); NASA/Visible Earth, 12 (Earth); Photodisc, 12 (Mercury);
Shutterstock/coko, 1; Shutterstock/CyMaN, 6; Shutterstock/IoanaDrutu, 20;
Shutterstock/Steven Dern, 18; SOHO (ESA & NASA), cover, 8